BRITAIN in WORLD WAR II

LIFE IN BRITAIN

Peter Hepplewhite

FRANKLIN WATTS
LONDON•SYDNEY

© 2003 Franklin Watts

First published in 2003 by
Franklin Watts
96 Leonard Street
London
EC2A 4XD

Franklin Watts Australia
45-51 Huntley Street
Alexandria
NSW 2015

ISBN: 0 7496 4874 0

A CIP catalogue record for this book is available from the British Library

Printed in Malaysia
Planning and production by Discovery Books Limited
Editor: Helen Dwyer
Design: Keith Williams
Picture Research: Rachel Tisdale

Photographs:
Cover and title page London Borough of Wandsworth, 5 top Robert Opie Collection,
5 bottom Hulton-Deutsch Collection/CORBIS, 6, 8, 9 top, 9 bottom, 10, 13 top & 13
bottom Imperial War Museum, 14 Bettmann/CORBIS, 15 top & 16 Imperial War
Museum, 17 top & 17 bottom Robert Opie Collection, 18 Public Records Office, 19
top Bettmann/CORBIS, 19 bottom, 20 top, 20 bottom, 21, 22, 23 top, 23 bottom &
24 Imperial War Museum, 25 Péter Hepplewhite, 26 Imperial War Museum, 27 Peter
Hepplewhite, 28 Imperial War Museum, 29 top & 29 bottom Discovery Picture
Library/Alex Ramsay

LIFE IN BRITAIN

BRITAIN in WORLD WAR II

Contents

Going to War

In 1933 the German people voted for a leader named Adolf Hitler. Germany had been defeated in World War I (1914-18) and Hitler promised to make his country great again.

Soon Hitler was threatening the rest of Europe. In March 1938 German troops marched into neighbouring Austria and six months later Hitler claimed the Sudetenland, a region in Czechoslovakia where many German people lived. The British Prime Minister, Neville Chamberlain, flew to meet Hitler in Munich and agreed to Hitler's terms, provided that he made no more territorial demands. An uneasy calm lasted until March 1939 when German troops marched into the rest of Czechoslovakia.

▶ Germany took over Austria and Sudetenland before the war. By 1942 Germany and its allies were at the height of their power, controlling most of Europe and North Africa.

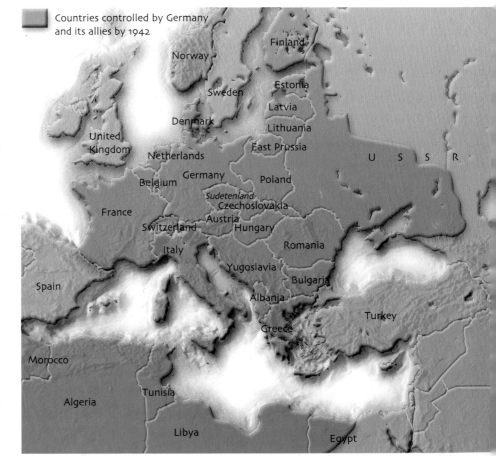

Countries controlled by Germany and its allies by 1942

Finland
Norway
Sweden
Estonia
Latvia
Denmark
Lithuania
United Kingdom
East Prussia
Netherlands
U S S R
Germany
Belgium
Poland
France
Sudetenland
Czechoslovakia
Switzerland
Austria
Hungary
Italy
Romania
Yugoslavia
Spain
Bulgaria
Albania
Turkey
Greece
Morocco
Algeria
Tunisia
Libya
Egypt

War is declared

Most British people now realised that Hitler had to be stopped. And they didn't have long to wait. At 11:15 am, on Sunday 3 September 1939, Chamberlain spoke on the radio. Germany had attacked Poland and the British government had declared war. 'It is evil things we are fighting against,' he said 'brute force, bad faith, injustice, **oppression** and persecution.'

Preparing for war

Chamberlain broadcast to a nation on the move. Everywhere families were torn apart as young men joined the **armed forces** and women and children hurriedly left the cities. There was a flood of weddings as couples decided to snatch time together, however short it might be.

Hitler will send no warning – so always carry your gas mask

ISSUED BY THE MINISTRY OF HOME SECURITY

▲ Forty million gas masks were issued to protect people from poisonous gas attacks. In the end neither side used this terrible weapon.

▶ Winston Churchill giving his famous V for Victory sign.

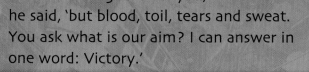

WINSTON CHURCHILL

Winston Churchill took over as Prime Minister in May 1940, when the German army was storming through France. He bluntly told the British people that the war would be long and hard. 'I have nothing to offer you,' he said, 'but blood, toil, tears and sweat. You ask what is our aim? I can answer in one word: Victory.'

World War II was soon called 'the People's War' because winning depended on everyone working hard to supply the armed services. Civilian life in Britain was known as the 'Home Front.' And for the first time, civilians were often in as much danger from air raids as soldiers were in battle.

Evacuation

Most people believed that the war would begin with massive attacks by enemy aircraft dropping bombs. To save lives, preparations were made to move millions of mothers, children and disabled people out of the industrial cities into the safety of the countryside.

Plans for the Evacuation Scheme, as it was known, were ready by the summer of 1939 and swung into action on 1 September. In three days 1.5 million people took part in the official evacuation and another 2 million made their own arrangements to stay with friends or relatives. Some 750,000 children were evacuated in school parties led by their teachers. Most travelled by train from the nearest station, carrying **gas masks**, lunches, backpacks of clothes and sometimes a much-loved toy.

▼A party of young city children is evacuated by train in 1939. The labels they are wearing have their names, school numbers and destinations written on them, in case they are lost on the busy platforms.

Urban poverty uncovered

When the evacuees arrived in the reception areas, **billeting officers** found them homes with families who had volunteered to be foster parents. But many hosts were in for a shock! Thousands of city children lived in poverty. They were infested with fleas and lice, and their clothes were often in tatters. Some had never seen a bathroom before or slept in clean sheets.

The bombing begins

By Christmas 1939 many evacuees had returned home. German bombers had not attacked yet and parents wanted their children back with them. But this quiet time did not last. In the summer of 1940 a massive German bombing campaign – the Blitz – began and there was a second evacuation with a million mothers and children leaving London and other big cities. The last evacuation came in the summer of 1944 when new bombs – V-1 and V-2 rockets – fell on London and the South East.

EVACUEE TALES

First bath

One little girl on having a bath remarked: 'It's the first time I have been washed all over at once – but it's nice.'

Sunderland Echo, *20 September 1939*

Farmhouse cooking

'The cooking was wonderful and I can remember how amazed I was to see apple pies and egg custards that were four or five inches (10-12 cm) deep. Farmhouse cooking of course!'

Betty Goodyear, evacuated from Birmingham to Wales

▲ At first gas masks were a great joke with children – they looked a bit like Mickey Mouse, the cartoon character. But it soon became a burden having to carry them everywhere, in case of a sudden gas attack.

Civil Defence

The British government was very worried about enemy bombers. During the Spanish Civil War (1936-39), deaths and injuries from air raids had been dreadfully high.

Based on this evidence, top experts forecast 25,000 dead in London alone during the first month of a war with Germany – and over a million if the fighting lasted a long time.

Thankfully they were wrong. German bombers could not carry such heavy loads of bombs as the experts had predicted and most of those dropped missed their targets. Even so, 60,000 civilians died in air raids during the war.

Air Raid Precautions

In 1935 every local council had to draw up an **Air Raid Precautions** (ARP) plan. By the end of 1938, 1.5 million adults had volunteered for **civil defence** work. By the time enemy raids began, every street or block had a warden who shepherded people to and from shelters when the sirens sounded. The alert siren was a long piercing wail while the all-clear was a loud warble. When bombs fell, the wardens telephoned reports to local control rooms. ARP Control then directed the fire, ambulance, rescue or first-aid squads to the most urgent incidents.

The blackout

Wardens had the very unpopular job of checking the **blackout**. From 1 September 1939 street lights were turned off and anyone showing a light at night was breaking the law.

▲Two women fire-fighters operating a hand-powered stirrup pump to spray water on a small fire.

SHELTERS AT HOME

By September 1939 one and a half million Anderson shelters had been put up in gardens. They came as a kit of 14 corrugated iron sheets that had to be bolted together and covered with soil. Morrison shelters were indoor shelters for homes without gardens. They were strong steel cages 2m long and 1.5m high, and were often used as tables during the day.

One lady in Sunderland was fined £3 – almost a week's wages – when she left a fire burning without drawing the curtains. Although the blackout made it harder for bombers to find their targets, the lack of lighting at night made life more difficult and dangerous for everyone.

▼ Anderson shelters were covered with earth to protect them from bomb blasts. Flowers and even vegetables could be grown on top of them.

▼ Sleeping in a Morrison shelter. If the house collapsed the people in the shelter might be unharmed, but many were simply buried alive.

The Home Guard

On Tuesday 14 May 1940 the government made an urgent appeal on the radio to all men aged between 17 and 65. The Germans had attacked Belgium and the Netherlands using soldiers dropped by parachutes.

To protect Britain, a new part-time force was to be set up, the Local Defence Volunteers (LDV), or 'Home Guard' as it was soon known. Within 24 hours a quarter of a million men had volunteered. By the end of July this number had risen to over a million.

Unprepared and ill-equipped

In June the British army was rescued from the beaches of Dunkirk in France, but the soldiers had to leave their equipment behind. The Home Guard found itself in the front line against a German invasion. At first they had few proper weapons. Old rifles from World War I were shared among three or four men, while others made do with shotguns, walking sticks, golf clubs, or knives fastened to broom handles. Uniforms consisted of khaki armbands.

◀ A Home Guard unit with a machine gun mounted in a motorcycle side car. The men are practising fighting in their gas masks.

Old soldiers became officers, and training took place in church halls or parks. No wonder the LDV soon earned the nicknames 'Look, Duck and Vanish' or 'Last Desperate Venture'.

The Home Guard at work

Despite these problems the Home Guard did valuable work. They defended key targets like factories, explosives stores, beaches and sea fronts. At night they patrolled fields in which enemy gliders or paratroops might land. No one expected them to beat well-trained German soldiers. Their job was to slow them down until the army arrived.

SECRET ARMY

The Home Guard also had a secret section – the Auxiliary Unit. If the Germans invaded and won, this handpicked force was to set up a resistance movement, striking from hidden bases in the countryside. They were specially trained in **guerrilla** fighting – ambushes, hand-to-hand fighting and **sabotage**. They were sworn to secrecy and most never told even their own families they were anything other than ordinary Home Guards.

▼ An aircraft spotter in London, 1940.

The Blitz

At 4:56 pm on 7 September 1940, the sirens wailed as the German Air Force, the Luftwaffe, launched a massive raid on London. Over 350 bombers flew across the Channel from airfields in France and dropped 300 tonnes of bombs on the docks and streets of the East End of the city.

Warehouses storing paint, rubber, rum, tea and sugar burst into flames. For most men and women in the **Auxiliary Fire Service** it was their first test. The bombers came again that night and 450 Londoners died. It was the start of the Blitz, 11 weeks when London was bombed every day or night, bar one.

▼ The East End of London burns after the first mass German air raid, 7 September 1940.

LONDON'S BURNING

On the first day of the Blitz fire-fighters faced horrific conditions tackling the East End warehouse fires. Hot sugar melted and burned on the water in the docks; rum barrels exploded like bombs; rubber burned with thick black smoke that choked anyone who went too close; thousands of rats fled the burning grain stores.

Bombing spreads to other cities

As autumn drew on the Germans
attacked other cities. The worst raid
struck Coventry on the night of
14 November 1940. Some 450 bombers
dropped 500 tonnes of high explosive
and 880 **incendiary** bombs. Thousands
of homes, two hospitals and 21 major
factories were hit. Most of the town
centre, including the ancient cathedral,
was destroyed. At least 550 people died
and 865 were seriously injured. In the spring of 1941
there were heavy raids in the West Midlands, Merseyside
and Clydebank in Glasgow. In Clydebank only 8 houses
out of 12,000 were left undamaged and 55,000 people
were made homeless.

▲ Bomb damage in Clapham,
London. The power lines for
the electric trolley buses have
been cut.

Morale remains high

Hitler hoped the bombing campaign
would break British **morale,** but all the
deaths and damage only made people
more determined to fight on. Even in
hard-hit Coventry a local pride soon
grew out of the rubble. A visitor at the
end of November wrote: 'Having got
over the first shock, I think the people
are now prepared to stand anything.'

▶ In London the Underground became a vast
emergency air raid shelter. On the busiest night
in 1940, 177,000 people slept on platforms.
Many brought sandwiches, thermos flasks,
pillows and blankets. In this photo even the
escalators are full.

Enemies at Home

In the 1920s and 1930s many people from Europe settled in Britain. Some were migrants looking for a better way of life while others were fleeing persecution. By September 1939 over 60,000 had fled from Germany and Austria, many of them Jews escaping persecution in Germany.

When the war began Britain's behaviour to these new arrivals was often harsh. They were classed as 'enemy aliens' and investigated by local police or intelligence officers in case they were spies, traitors or **saboteurs**.

Spy fever

In the summer of 1940, when invasion seemed likely, Britain was gripped by spy fever. All German men between the ages of 16 and 60 were prime suspects. On 16 May, in an early morning swoop, 2,000 were arrested in London. In June Italy declared war on Britain and Italians were added to the list. Mobs attacked Italian restaurants and many Italian families were put into custody. Victor Tollani, a waiter, had lived in England since he was a boy. When he was marched away by the police he heard a teacher say to his pupils: 'Look at the dirty Germans! Spit at them!' He remembered being upset when the children did as they were told, but even more hurt at being called a German.

◀ These Jewish refugee children escaped from Germany in 1938 and stayed in a holiday camp in Essex.

BRITISH SUSPECTS

Over 1,600 British citizens were interned too, most of them members of the British Union of **Fascists** (BUF). The BUF was set up and led by Sir Oswald Mosley. The BUF wanted Britain to be an ally of Germany. Members wore a black shirt as their uniform and copied the Nazi raised arm salute. Mosley had been married in Berlin in 1936 and Hitler was a guest at his wedding.

Internment and curfews

Many of those arrested were sent to **internment camps,** even though they hadn't committed any crimes. Several camps were on the Isle of Man, as far as possible from German-occupied Europe. Those aliens left free were subject to a **curfew.** They had to be home by midnight and couldn't go out before 6 am.

▼ Everyone in Britain was issued with an Identity Card and had to carry it with them all the time.

CARRY YOUR IDENTITY CARD ALWAYS

NATIONAL REGISTRATION IDENTITY D

YOU MAY BE ASKED FOR IT AT ANY TIME TO PROVE TO THE POLICE OR MILITARY WHO YOU ARE & WHERE YOU LIVE

Your card must bear your usual address. If you move go to the National Registration Office and have the address altered there. You must not alter the address yourself or anything else on your card.

◀ Thousands of German and Italian prisoners of war were kept in camps in Britain. From the summer of 1941 many were used as workers on farms, often unguarded. This photo shows a group of British women and Italian prisoners working on a farm in Herefordshire.

Making Do

In 1939 Britain was one of the greatest trading nations in the world. Merchant ships crossed the seas bringing goods of all kinds, from potatoes to petrol. But by the end of 1940 German submarines called U-boats were sinking so many British merchant ships that the country faced starvation.

Key foods such as flour, meat and sugar were in such short supply that they were **rationed**. Everyone was issued with a ration book that contained coupons. When an item was paid for, the shopkeeper took out the correct number of coupons. This meant that no one could buy more than their fair share. New foods such as dried eggs, SPAM (tins of spiced pork and ham) and even whale meat became common.

Growing more food

The only way to beat the U-boats was for Britain to grow more food. Farmers ploughed up grassland and moors to sow wheat, oats and potatoes. The government's Dig for Victory campaign encouraged people to plant fruit and vegetables instead of flowers in their gardens.

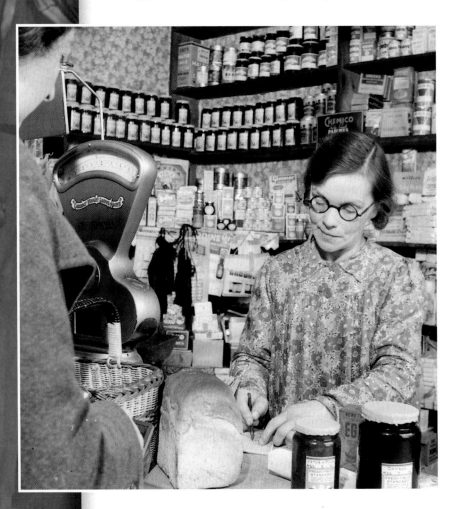

◀ A shopkeeper marks a purchase in a customer's ration book.

Sadie MacDougal worked in a **munitions** factory in Newcastle. She remembered: 'For a pair of stockings it was three coupons, so we painted our legs. We got a straight line up the back, like a pair of fully fashioned stockings, only in paint. We used to sweetheart some of the boys from the drawing office who could draw nice and straight.'

Parks, playing fields and roadside verges – even the lawns of Buckingham Palace – were turned into vegetable plots. Families reared pigs, chickens and rabbits in their gardens to slaughter for meat. Recipes for delicacies like carrot jam, cabbage stalk soup and stale bread pudding helped to cut any waste.

Clothes rationed too

Clothes rationing began in June 1941 and soon it became fashionable to be shabbily dressed. Churchill set the tone by appearing in public in overalls. Everyone was allowed 60 clothing coupons a year. A man's coat used up 15 and a pair of shoes 5.

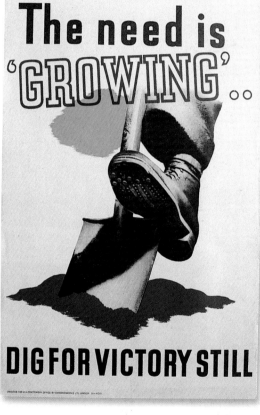

▲ This poster called on gardeners to Dig for Victory so that Britain wouldn't starve.

▲ People were told that it was their duty to save resources of all kinds, including water, coal, electricity and gas. Some posters claimed that any sort of waste was a help to Hitler!

Industry at War

Prime Minister Churchill knew that if Britain was to survive, the armed forces needed an endless supply of munitions. The costs, however, were huge.

In 1943 alone factories turned out 29,800 tanks; 900,000 rifles; 7,000 anti-aircraft guns; 26,000 aircraft; and 100,000 machine guns to arm the troops. Between 1939 and June 1944 British shipyards built over 700 major warships and over 6,000 merchant ships.

Stricter work laws

Ernest Bevin became Minister of Labour in 1940. He was put in charge of making sure every essential industry had enough workers.

Under strict new laws, all men and women had to register for work. Bevin had the power to order them to do any job, anywhere in the country. One example was mining. All industries depended on coal for electricity but by 1943 there was a shortage of miners. To meet this demand 21,000 young men were told to go into the mines rather than join the army.

The big raids on Germany continue. British war plants share with the R.A.F. credit for these giant operations.

THE ATTACK BEGINS IN THE FACTORY

◀ Posters like this encouraged workers by showing the importance of the weapons they made for winning the war.

THE WOODEN WONDER

The Mosquito bomber was nicknamed the 'Wooden Wonder' by Royal Air Force crews. It was also a triumph of British engineering. The **fuselage** and wings were made of wood at a time when most other aircraft needed scarce aluminium. Better still, the Mosquito was assembled by a different workforce – furniture makers, shop fitters and caravan builders – at a time when there was a desperate shortage of metal workers. Lightweight and fitted with two Rolls-Royce Merlin engines, the Mosquito could outrun the fastest German fighters.

Making munitions

Thousands of factories switched from making peacetime goods to munitions. Littlewoods, the mail order firm in Liverpool, began to make **barrage balloons,** while the Bryant and May match factory in London produced **fuses** for demolition work. Other factories were specially built, like the giant munitions plant at Chorley near Manchester. This employed 35,000 people.

◀ Women making barrels for artillery at a British munitions factory, July 1941.

Women at War

One of the great success stories of the war was the vital work done by women. By 1943 all women between the ages of 18 and 51 were liable for war service, if they didn't have children at home. Some went into the armed forces but most took over vital jobs in industry, farming, transport and civil defence.

◀ Although women were not allowed to fight 450,000 joined the armed forces. Members of the Women's Auxiliary Air Force became mechanics, drivers, radar operators and even pilots delivering planes to squadrons. Women in the army joined the Auxiliary Territorial Service and those in the navy the Women's Royal Naval Service. The women in this photograph were pilots in the Air Transport Auxiliary.

Over 1.5 million extra women went to work in essential industries. These included engineering, chemical production, shipbuilding and steel-making. Often the women tackled jobs that were traditionally men's work, such as welding or operating **machine tools.**

▶ Women who couldn't work were encouraged to help the war effort by looking after workers' children.

If *you* can't go to the factory help the neighbour who *can*

How you can help

Arrange now with a neighbour to look after her children when she goes to her war-work—or give your name to

CARING FOR WAR WORKERS' CHILDREN IS A NATIONAL SERVICE

In peacetime Helen Bliss had run a small restaurant, but in 1942 she trained to make aircraft parts in a factory in Croydon, in Surrey. Helen worked 12 hours a day, six days a week – and all night if there was an urgent order.

Hard work and poor pay

Factory conditions were frequently hard, dirty and dangerous. And all too often men saw the women as a threat. In one Birmingham factory the men on night shift objected to their **lathes** being used by the women on day shift and loosened all the nuts on the machines when they went home! Not only was this unsafe, it meant that the women wasted time the next day fixing the lathes.

Few women were paid the same as men, even if their jobs were identical. In the armed forces women were paid a third less than men and given smaller portions of food.

▲ Over 80,000 women became 'Land Girls'. They lived on farms doing everything from planting potatoes and repairing tractors to rat-catching and tree-felling. Their wages were among the lowest in the country. These Land Girls were photographed on a forestry training course in Culford, Suffolk.

DANGER ... AND BOREDOM

Half a million women volunteered for Civil Defence. Theodora Benson was an ARP driver during the Blitz. She recalled: 'There were nights filled with the drama of driving through cratered and blacked-out streets to dig people and parts of people out of bombed buildings. In contrast other nights were spent bored, bickering, joking, grumbling and having fun.'

The Yanks

Britain was invaded during the war – by friendly Allies! Tens of thousands of fighting men from all over German-occupied Europe and the British Empire flocked to defend Britain.

They included Poles, Czechs, Free French, Indians, Australians, Canadians and New Zealanders. It was the Americans, however, who made the biggest impact. The United States of America entered the war in December 1941, after the Japanese attacked Pearl Harbor, an American base in the Pacific.

▼American servicemen in London are given a free Thanksgiving Day turkey dinner. Small gestures like this made lonely or homesick men feel a little better.

By June 1944 there were over 1,400,000 US soldiers and another 426,000 airmen in the Britain. In a huge construction programme, hundreds of army camps and airbases were built in quiet country areas. A typical airfield needed a concrete runway a mile (1.6 km) long; two smaller back-up runways; 50 kilometres of drains; 500 separate buildings; and a sewerage plant for 2,500 people. So many US troops were based in the county of Wiltshire that by 1944 there was one American for every two British civilians.

The glamorous GIs

The Americans were nicknamed 'Yanks', or 'GIs' because their kit was marked 'Government Issue'. To most war-weary people in Britain, they seemed incredibly glamorous, like Hollywood film stars.

GOT ANY GUM, CHUM?

GIs were always surrounded by children yelling, 'Got any gum, chum?' The fast reply to this was 'Gotta sister, mister?' Always keen to foster good relations, the US Air Force laid on parties for more than 60,000 British children between 1942 and 1944.

▼ American soldiers throw a party for 200 British children in London, November 1942.

GIs were paid five times as much as British troops and it seemed that the stores on every American base sold an endless supply of luxury goods: fruit, butter, chocolate, ice-cream, nylon stockings, lipstick and scented soap. No wonder the Yanks became popular boyfriends for British women! After the war 34,000 'GI brides' went back to the USA with their new American husbands.

▼ 'GI brides' (British women who had married American servicemen) leaving Southampton at the end of the war to join their husbands in the USA.

Adoption and racism

Many British families took up the offer to become 'foster parents' and 'adopt' a Yank. One aspect of the American forces caused problems however – racism. Black GIs had to live in separate camps and visit British pubs and cinemas on different days from white servicemen.

Entertainment

When the war started the government ordered all cinemas, dance halls and places of public entertainment to be closed down. Most of these controls were lifted within a few weeks after a wave of complaints. People needed to relax, and entertainment was vital for morale.

▲ Comedian and singer George Formby entertaining Londoners taking shelter in Aldwych tube station, during the Blitz.

Going to the pictures was a hugely popular pastime. Over 30 million visits were made each week during the Blitz (September 1940-May 1941). Queuing for two hours was not uncommon so customers had to be patient. Cinemas often showed **patriotic** films. Some were set in wartime; others looked to Britain's glorious past. But the most popular movies were from Hollywood: love stories, gangster adventures or musicals that helped audiences forget their hardships for a few hours.

Wartime shows

ENSA, the Entertainments National Service Association, hired stars to give free shows all over the country. Venues included public air raid shelters and aircraft hangars.

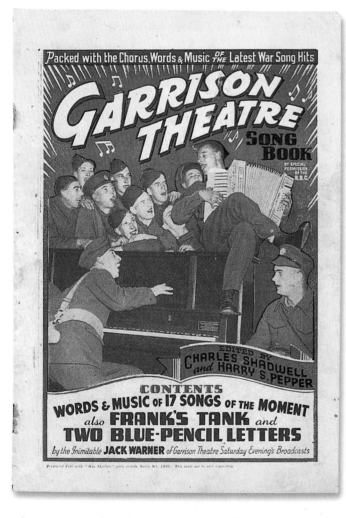

▲ Garrison Theatre was a popular radio programme starring Jack Warner. This song sheet helped people to have a 'sing-along' at home.

In 1940 ENSA presented 200 concerts in factories. By 1944 this had risen to an amazing 2,200. Many shows were broadcast on the radio in a programme called 'Workers' Playtime'. Stars included comedians like Max Miller and George Formby, or popular singers like the Andrews Sisters and Vera Lynn.

Radio entertainment

The blackout and petrol rationing made travelling difficult, so entertainment at home became important. Sales of radio sets boomed and every week around 16 million people tuned into the comedy 'ITMA' (It's That Man Again), starring Tommy Handley. Based in his Office of Twerps in the Ministry of Aggravation, Tommy made fun of the wartime regulations that irritated ordinary people.

The Will to Win

From the outbreak of war the government used all kinds of advertising to convince the British people that they could win.

The Ministry of Information was in charge of this propaganda and also controlled what newspapers and the radio were allowed to say about the fighting. Across the country billboards were plastered with posters, leaflets were pushed through doors and cinemas showed government information films before the main features.

▲ The most effective ideas often used humour. The devilish Squander Bug, stamped with swastikas – symbols of Germany's ruling Nazi party – nagged housewives to waste money.

Churchill's speeches

In the darkest days of 1940 the brilliant speeches of Winston Churchill stoked the fighting spirit of the country. Whenever he spoke on the radio, seven out of ten people listened. After the Germans conquered France in May, he made a rousing declaration: 'We shall defend our island, whatever the cost may be. We shall fight on the beaches, we shall fight on the landing grounds, we shall fight in the fields and in the streets, we shall fight in the hills. We shall never surrender.'

Raising money

One of the longest government campaigns focused on National Savings – convincing people to buy War Savings Certificates so the government could use the money to pay for the war. Special appeals included War Weapons Weeks in 1941; Wings for Victory in 1943; and Salute the Soldier in 1944. Every local community became involved with parades, dances, touring cinema vans and sports tournaments, encouraging people to buy savings certificates.

▶ Tynemouth had a tough savings target for Salute the Soldier Week 1944 – £500,000 – enough to equip an infantry brigade.

LORD HAW HAW

Millions regularly tuned in their radios to listen to the German broadcasts of William Joyce. Joyce was a supporter of Hitler and tried to convince his British audience that they were losing the war. An Irish American, he mimicked a posh English accent with his opening words 'Jairmany calling.' Most listeners made fun of his voice and gave him the nickname 'Lord Haw Haw'. He was hanged for treason in 1946.

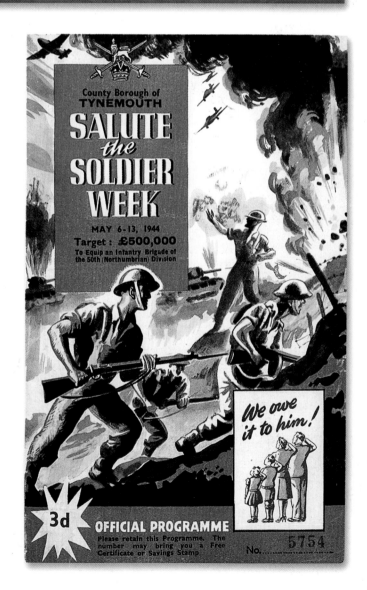

Remembering the War

On 30 April 1945 Adolf Hitler shot himself and a few days later Germany surrendered. Victory in Europe (VE) Day was celebrated on 8 May with parties, parades and fireworks across the country.

One girl remembered: 'Our street had a great big party and everyone painted their houses red, white and blue. My Auntie Al got her piano outside and everyone was dancing and singing. The party went on all night.'

Soon the troops started to come home. Thirty thousand men and women were demobbed (sent home) each week and by December 1945 over a million had left the services. Many men returned to children who only knew 'Dad' from a photograph.

◀ The Channel Islands were the only part of the British Isles occupied by the Germans. When the enemy surrendered the islanders went wild with delight. This house is in Saint Peter Port on Guernsey.

◀ The medieval cathedral in Coventry was destroyed by German bombs in 1940. The new cathedral built after the war has become a symbol of forgiveness and friendship between Britain and Germany.

▶ Local war memorials, such as this one in Monmouth, record the dead from both world wars: World War I (1914-18) and World War II (1939-45).

Museums tell the story

Today World War II is history. But one of the best ways to learn about life in those turbulent years is to see them for yourself. All over the country museums have preserved key wartime sites and objects from the time, such as gas masks and ration books.

Local reminders of the war

Closer to home you can visit community war memorials and read the names of those who died. Your local library will probably have photographs of wartime bomb damage and may keep a list of any nearby fortifications. Machine-gun posts and gun emplacements were built of thick concrete and often still survive because they are too difficult to demolish!

Best of all make your own wartime history. Talk to servicemen and civilians who lived through World War II and record their unique story.

Timeline

1939
September: Blackout introduced and evacuation begins; Britain declares war on Germany.

1940
January: Food rationing begins.

May: Churchill become Prime Minister; Local Defence Volunteers formed.

September: Blitz on London begins.

November: Air raid on Coventry.

1941
March-May: German U-boats sink 142 merchant ships.

June: Clothes rationing begins.

December: America joins the war against Germany, Italy and Japan.

1942
January: First American troops arrive.

1943
May: Women aged 18-45 called up for war work.

December: 21,000 men sent to work in mines.

1944
June: D-Day invasion of Europe from Britain.

June: First German flying bomb attacks on Britain.

December: Home Guard disbanded.

1945
May: Germany surrenders; VE day celebrations.

Places to Visit

390th Bomb Group Memorial Air Museum, Parham Airfield, Parham, Woodbridge, Suffolk
Explore a US Air Force airfield.

Eden Camp, Malton, North Yorkshire
Discover more about everyday life on the Home Front.

German Occupation Museum, Forest, Guernsey, Channel Islands
Discover what it was like to be ruled by the Germans.

HMS *Belfast*, Morgan's Lane, London
Step aboard a World War II cruiser.

Royal Air Force Air Defence Radar Museum, RAF Neatishead, Norwich
Explore a 1942 ground-controlled interception room.

Royal Scots Regimental Museum, The Castle, Edinburgh
Find out what the oldest regiment in the army did during the war.

Stockport Air Raid Shelters, 61 Chestergate, Stockport
Visit original wartime bomb shelters.

The Tank Museum, Bovington, Dorset
Visit the finest collection of World War II tanks in the country, including the awesome German Tiger tank.

Western Approaches, 1 Rumford Street, Liverpool
Find out how the German U-boats (submarines) were beaten.

Imperial War Museum, Lambeth Road, London
Covers all aspects of life in wartime, at home and on the battlefield.

Imperial War Museum, Duxford, Cambridgeshire
A large aviation museum with World War II planes that still fly at air shows.

Cabinet War Rooms, King Charles Street, London
Where Winston Churchill, his ministers and top military personnel met and sheltered during the war. Explore the map room, the cabinet room and the room where Churchill slept.

Portsmouth D-Day Museum, Portsmouth
Experience the sights and sounds of Britain at war with reminiscences of local people, and find out about the D-Day landings of 1944.

Glossary

Air Raid Precautions (ARP) organisation and personnel that protected and rescued people during bomb attacks from the air.

armed forces army, navy and air force.

Auxiliary Fire Service men and women who volunteered to serve as an emergency fire brigade.

barrage balloons gas filled balloons tethered to the ground by steel cables, to cut the wings off low flying enemy bombers.

billeting officers officials in charge of finding accommodation for evacuees.

blackout covering all windows and turning off all lights at night so that no lights showed to enemy aircraft.

civil defence looking after ordinary people during wartime. ARP later became known as Civil Defence.

curfew a time after which people must stay indoors until the next morning.

fascist somebody who believes their country should be run by an all-powerful government or dictator with no opposition.

fuses devices that set off an explosive.

fuselage the body of a plane.

gas mask a mask with a filter to help a person breathe during an attack by poisonous gas.

guerrilla a person who fights using 'hit and run' tactics.

incendiary small bomb that starts a fire when it explodes.

internment camps camps used to lock up people who are suspected of helping the enemy.

lathes turning machines on which metal or wood can be shaped.

machine tools machines that make precise parts for other machines.

morale the way people feel about a war, and whether they think their side can win.

munitions weapons and ammunition.

oppression control by force.

patriotic supporting your country.

ration share out goods in short supply so no-one has more than anyone else.

sabotage damaging equipment or machinery.

saboteur someone who damages equipment or machinery to help the enemy.

Books and Websites

Books

Asa Briggs, *Go To It*, Mitchell Beazley, 2000

Alan Childs, *A Day in the Life of a World War II Evacuee*, Wayland, 2000

Peter Hepplewhite, *My War: Evacuees*, Hodder Wayland, 2003

Peter Hepplewhite, *My War: RAF*, Hodder Wayland, 2003

Rebecca Hunter and Angela Downey, *Grandma's War*, Evans, 1999

Stewart Ross, *On the Trail of World War II in Britain*, Franklin Watts, 1999

Rachel Wright, *World War II: facts, things to make, activities*, Franklin Watts, 2001

Websites
www.iwm.org.uk
This Imperial War Museum site is the gateway to five top museums, including Churchill's top secret Cabinet War Rooms.

www. war-experience.org
The Second World War Experience Centre is a site devoted to the personal memories of war veterans.

www.spartacus.schoolnet.co.uk/2WW.htm
A great World War II encyclopaedia.

www.bbc.co.uk/history/ww2children
Find out what life was like for children during World War II.

Index